100 MCQs ON
CRADLE to CONFIDENCE 21st CENTURY PARENTING SKILLS

DR CLARENCE PETER

MA (Eng, Eco, Edu) BEd, MBA (Exe), PhD (Edu Mgt)

DR MALAY RANJAN PATI

MA (History) Utkal Univ, PhD

(Broadcast Journalism in India) Utkal Univ

notionpress
.com

INDIA • SINGAPORE • MALAYSIA

"CRADLE TO CONFIDENCE:

21ST CENTURY PARENTING STYLES"

… explores modern approaches to raising confident and resilient children in today's fast-paced world. This comprehensive guide examines the evolving dynamics of PARENTING, blending traditional wisdom with contemporary insights. It delves into various PARENTING STYLES, highlighting the importance of fostering independence, emotional intelligence, and adaptability. Through practical tips, the book addresses challenges such as screen time management, academic pressures, and social media influence. It emphasizes the role of nurturing a child's self-esteem and confidence from infancy through adolescence. **"CRADLE TO CONFIDENCE — 21ST CENTURY PARENTING STYLES"** aims to equip parents with the tools and knowledge needed to support their children's growth into well-rounded individuals, capable of thriving in the 21st century. Whether you are a new parent or navigating the teenage years, this book offers valuable guidance for every stage of your parenting journey.

… a comprehensive guide for modern parents navigating the complexities of raising children in today's fast-paced world. Your book merges time-tested parenting wisdom with cutting-edge experience to provide practical, effective strategies for fostering confident, resilient children. We delve into diverse parenting styles, addressing the unique challenges of the digital age, from managing screen time to coping with academic pressures and social media influences. Your book equips you with the tools to support your child's emotional and intellectual growth. Whether you're a new parent or guiding teenagers, **"CRADLE TO CONFIDENCE — 21ST CENTURY PARENTING STYLES"** offers invaluable advice to help your children thrive. Join us on this journey to nurture well-rounded individuals, ready to face the future with confidence and adaptability. Let's embark on this transformative adventure together, shaping the leaders of tomorrow and better citizens of our country…

WHY? READ THIS BOOK

"CRADLE TO CONFIDENCE - -
21ST CENTURY PARENTING STYLES"

1. **Comprehensive Guidance**: Provides in-depth information on a variety of modern PARENTING STYLES, offering a well-rounded perspective and incorporates advice from child development experts and psychologists, ensuring our readers to receive credible and up-to-date parenting styles;

2. **Practical Tips**: Offers actionable strategies that parents can implement immediately to enhance their parenting skills with real life experiences that illustrate key concepts and solutions;

3. **Screen Time Management**: Addresses the challenges of screen time, providing effective ways to balance use of technology;

4. **Emotional Intelligence**: Emphasizes the importance of developing your child's emotional intelligence which is crucial for their social and personal growth;

5. **Confidence Building**: Focuses on nurturing a child's self-esteem and confidence from infancy through adolescence;

6. **Adaptability**: Teaches parents how to raise adaptable and resilient children in an ever-changing world;

7. **Work-Life Balance**: Offers advice on maintaining a healthy work-life balance while being actively involved in children's lives;

8. **Future-Proofing**: Prepares parents and children for future challenges by fostering Critical Thinking, Problem-Solving, and independence.

WHY MCQs FORMAT?

Multiple Choice Questions (MCQs) offer several advantages in various contexts in making Parenting a successful one ... ...

1. **EFFICIENCY AND TIME - SAVING:**

   Quick Assessment: MCQs allow for rapid evaluation of knowledge and understanding. They can cover a wide range of content in a short period, making them efficient for both Parents and Child(ren);

2. **OBJECTIVE MEASUREMENT:**

   Clear Feedback: Immediate feedback is often possible with MCQs, helping Parents to quickly identify areas of strength and weakness;

3. **VERSATILITY AND COMPREHENSIVE COVERAGE:**

   Variety of Topics: MCQs can be used to assess knowledge across diverse subjects and topics, making them versatile for different Parenting Styles;

4. **ENHANCED LEARNING AND RETENTION:**

   Focus on Key Concepts: MCQs can highlight and reinforce important concepts, helping Parents to focus on the most critical information.

5. **DIAGNOSTIC TOOL:**

   Identifying Gaps: MCQs can help identify specific areas where Parents may have misunderstandings or knowledge gaps, guiding targeted instruction.

HOW TO PRACTICE

21ST CENTURY PARENTING STYLES —
"CRADLE TO CONFIDENCE

These practices aim to cultivate a nurturing and empowering environment where child(ren) can grow into confident and capable individuals:

1. **POSITIVE REINFORCEMENT**: Focus on praising and encouraging your child's efforts and achievements rather than solely on outcomes;

2. **EMOTIONAL COACHING**: Help your child identify and manage their emotions, teaching them empathy and resilience;

3. **BALANCED SCREEN TIME**: Set limits on technology use and encourage activities that promote physical, mental, and social development;

4. **EFFECTIVE COMMUNICATION**: Foster open and honest communication with your child, creating a supportive environment for discussing concerns and challenges;

5. **TEACHING INDEPENDENCE**: Gradually encourage your child to take on age-appropriate responsibilities, fostering confidence and self-reliance;

6. **SETTING BOUNDARIES**: Establish clear and consistent rules and consequences, helping your child understand expectations and boundaries;

7. **PROMOTING CURIOSITY**: Encourage exploration and curiosity, supporting your child's natural desire to learn and grow;

8. **BUILDING RELATIONSHIPS**: Help your child develop strong relationships with peers and adults, nurturing social skills and emotional intelligence;

9. **ENCOURAGING RESILIENCE**: Teach your child problem-solving skills and how to bounce back from setbacks, building resilience and adaptability;

10. **MODELLING BEHAVIOUR**: Be a positive role model by demonstrating kindness, respect, and integrity in your interactions, shaping your child's values and behaviours.

10 TRAITS OF
21ST CENTURY HIGHLY FFECTIVE PARENTS

1. **PARENTS AS COMMUNICATORS**:

YOU as highly effective PARENT is a COMMUNICATOR - a genuine and open person with the capacity to listen, empathize, and connect with your child(ren) in productive, helping and healing ways. YOU also have the ability to teach, present, and motivate them in larger groups.

YOU possess these QUALITIES:

- **Attend and listen to your child(ren)'s problems;**

- **Empathize and gets the whole story;**

- **Ask the right questions and say what they mean and mean what they say;**

- **Easily accept criticism and communicate creatively;**

- **Can disagree agreeably and connect in productive, helping and healing ways;**

2. PARENTS AS EDUCATORS:

YOU as highly effective PARENT is an EDUCATOR - a self-directed instructional leader with a strong intellect and knowledge regarding parenting, instruction and learning. YOU motivate and facilitate intellectual growth and development of self and your child(ren).

YOU possess these QUALITIES:

- **Believe that everyone can learn thus YOU develop programs to help them succeed and also provide training and support for your child(ren);**

- **Establish, implement and achieve academic standards;**

- **Focus on instruction and model continuous learning;**

- **Develop your child(ren) as leaders and pay close attention to what matters most;**

3. PARENTS AS ENVISIONERS:

YOU as highly effective PARENT is an ENVISIONER - an individual who has a focused vision of what your child(ren) can become and is motivated by a sense of calling and purpose.

YOU possess these QUALITIES:

- **Feel called and has resolve, goals, and life vision;**

- **Can see the invisible and know where your child(ren) are headed;**

- **Have compelling visions and can easily articulate your visions and then make them happen.**

4.   PARENTS AS FACILITATORS:

YOU as highly effective PARENT is a FACILITATOR - a leader with outstanding interpersonal relation skills that include the ability to build individual relationships with your own child(ren) and other parents.

YOU possess these QUALITIES:

- **Tap the potential of your child(ren) and build up emotional bonding;**

- **Say "We" instead of "I" and cultivate your own well-being;**

- **Value diversity and are basically positive person;**

- **Promote parental involvement and cheer lead and celebrate.**

5.   PARENTS AS CHANGE MASTERS:

YOU as highly effective PARENT is a CHANGE MASTER - a realistic, flexible and futuristic individual who is able to both motivate and manage change in an organized, positive, and enduring fashion amongst your child(ren) and other family members.

YOU possess these QUALITIES:

- **Handle uncertainty and ambiguity and use a situational approach;**

- **Respect resisters and know that the power is within;**

- **Value the plans and procedures and provide resources;**

- **Are willing to change yourself and are proactive motivator;**

- **Understand the change process and know that "small stuff" is really "big stuff.**

6. PARENTS AS CULTURE BUILDERS:

YOU as highly effective PARENT is a CULTURE BUILDER - an individual who models and communicates a strong and viable vision totally based on achievements, expectations, character, personal responsibility and accountability in the family.

YOU possess these QUALITIES:

- **Understand and appreciate the power of culture and thoroughly know what a good culture looks like;**

- **Facilitate the development of core values and communicates those values clearly;**

- **Reward and cheer those who support and build cultures that people choose.**

7. PARENTS AS ACTIVATORS:

The highly effective PARENT is an ACTIVATOR - an individual with energy, humour, drive, motivation and enthusiasm which is more than enough to spare and share with your own child(ren) and other family members.

YOU possess these QUALITIES:

- **Mobilize people and are entrepreneurial;**

- **Are risk taker and don't wait to be told to take any initiatives;**

- **Ask for forgiveness instead of permission and make things happen;**

- **Are outrageous and don't micromanage;**

- **Are cheer leader and run to daylight.**

8. PARENTS AS PRODUCERS:

The highly effective PARENT is a PRODUCER – YOU translate high expectations into intellectual development and academic achievement for your child(ren). You are a result-oriented individual with a strong sense of accountability to child(ren) and other members of the family. Producer like you believe that achievement is the bottom line.

YOU possess these QUALITIES:

- **Never mistake activity for achievement;**

- **Are data-driven and pay close attention to individuals in the family;**

- **Have academically focused missions and make research-based decisions.**

9. PARENTS AS CHARACTER BUILDERS:

The highly effective PARENT is a CHARACTER BUILDER – is a trustworthy person, has integrity, is authentic, shows respect, is generous and humble. A role model who values the words and deeds of one and all.

YOU possess these QUALITIES:

- **Are humane in nature and are trustworthy;**

- **Have integrity and are respectful;**

- **Hire others with character and are generous;**

- **Lead by example, not by exhortation and are authentic;**

- **Are consistent and seek to develop the character of your child(ren).**

10. PARENTS AS CONTRIBUTORS:

The highly effective PARENT is a CONTRIBUTOR – an encourager, a servant - leader and an enabler whose utmost priority is making contributions to the success of their child(ren) and other members in the family.

YOU possess this QUALITIES:

- **Lead by serving others and are self-aware and reflective;**

- **YOU pay full attention to your child's words and feelings and validate their emotions and build their confidence. This shows that their thoughts and feelings matter;**

- **You recognize and celebrate your child's efforts and achievements, big or small. You boosts their self-esteem and motivate them to continue striving for success.**

100 MCQs ON

"CRADLE TO CONFIDENCE:
21ST CENTURY PARENTING STYLES"

1. **What is a key characteristic of 21st-century Parenting?**

    (a) Authoritarianism

    (b) Neglect

    (c) Permissiveness

    (d) Helicopter Parenting

Answer: (d) HELICOPTER PARENTING

AN EXTRA MINUTE

HELICOPTER PARENTING refers to an over-involved parenting style where parents excessively monitor and intervene in their child(ren)'s lives. This can hinder the development of self-efficacy in child(ren). You can raise independent kids by balancing support and autonomy this also involves a delicate balance of guidance and freedom. By promoting decision-making, problem-solving, responsibility, self-regulation, practical skills, and self-confidence, you as parents can help your children develop the independence needed to thrive in a complex world.

"Children are not things to be moulded, but are people to be unfolded."

– (Jess Lair)

2. Which of the following is often emphasized in Parenting?

(a) Strict Discipline

(b) Child Independence

(c) Financial Success

(d) Parent-Centered Decision Making

Answer: (b) CHILD INDEPENDENCE

AN EXTRA MINUTE

CHILD INDEPENDENCE empowers child(ren) to become independent which is a vital aspect of their growth and development. You can help your child(ren) develop skills and confidence needed to become independent, capable individuals. This process not only benefits the child(ren) but also strengthens the parent-child relationship. You should highlight the importance to make age-appropriate decisions and take on responsibilities to build confidence and leadership skills and encourage Decision-Making by offering choices. Give children options to choose from various situations, such as selecting their clothes or choosing between activities.

"Parenting is not about being perfect, it's about being present."

– Unknown

3. **What technology is commonly used by parents to monitor their child(ren)?**

(a) Home Phones

(b) Social Media Apps

(c) GPS Tracking Devices

(d) Desktop Computers

Answer: (c) GPS TRACKING DEVICES

AN EXTRA MINUTE

GPS TRACKING DEVICES provides peace of mind by ensuring the safety and location of your children. It allows you to effectively monitor your child(ren)'s whereabouts in real-time through a smartphone app. Features often include geo-fencing, alerts for unscheduled movements, and emergency SOS buttons. It's a modern tool for enhancing your child's safety.

"The way we talk to our child(ren) becomes their inner voice."

– (Peggy O'Mara)

4. Which concept focuses on balancing Parental involvement and allowing child(ren) to learn from their own experiences?

(a) Authoritative Parenting

(b) Tiger Parenting

(c) Attachment Parenting

(d) Free-Range Parenting

Answer: (d) FREE - RANGE PARENTING

AN EXTRA MINUTE

FREE-RANGE PARENTING encourages child(ren) to explore and experience life with minimal adult supervision, promoting independence and self-reliance. You should now start trusting your child(ren) to make decisions, solve problems, and navigate their environment. It balances safety with freedom, fostering resilience and confidence. It's about giving kids the space to grow and learn naturally.

"To be in your child(ren)'s memories tomorrow,

you have to be in their lives today."

– (Barbara Johnson)

5.   **What is a common challenge faced by 21ˢᵗ Century Parents?**

(a)   Lack of Educational Resources

(b)   Balancing Work and Family Life

(c)   Finding Appropriate Childcare

(d)   Ensuring Proper Nutrition

Answer: (b) BALANCING WORK AND FAMILY LIFE

AN EXTRA MINUTE

BALANCING WORK AND FAMILY LIFE is essential for you to ensure harmony and well-being. Effective time management, setting priorities, and clear communication help achieve this balance. Flexibility in work hours or remote work options can reduce stress. You have to spend quality time with family, setting boundaries, and self-care. You have to strive for balance which will foster a positive home environment and support personal and professional fulfillment.

"Child(ren) need models rather than Critics."

– (Joseph Joubert)

6. **Which Parenting style is characterized by high responsiveness and high demands?**

(a) Authoritarian

(b) Permissive

(c) Authoritative

(d) Neglectful

Answer: (c) AUTHORITATIVE

AN EXTRA MINUTE

AUTHORITATIVE PARENTING balances high expectations with support and responsiveness. You should set clear rules and guidelines but also value open communication and understanding amongst your kids. This style fosters independence, self-discipline, and social responsibility in children. It combines firmness with warmth which encourages child(ren) to express their thoughts and feelings. Authoritative Parenting is associated with positive outcomes like academic success, emotional stability, and strong problem-solving skills.

"In raising my child(ren), I have lost my mind but found my soul."
– (Lisa T. Shepherd)

7. What is a major influence on 21st Century Parenting Styles?

(a) Religious Teachings

(b) Cultural Traditions

(c) Psychological Research

(d) Government Policies

Answer: (c) PSYCHOLOGICAL RESEARCH

AN EXTRA MINUTE

PSYCHOLOGICAL RESEARCH significantly influences parenting styles by providing insights into child(ren) development and behavior. Many studies highlight the impact of authoritative, authoritarian, permissive, and uninvolved parenting on a child's emotional and social growth. Research emphasizes the benefits of a balanced approach, combining warmth and structure. It guides you in adopting better effective strategies, fostering positive relationships, and promoting healthy development, leading to well-adjusted and resilient children.

"The best way to make child(ren) good is to make them happy."

– (Oscar Wilde)

8.   How has the internet impacted Parenting?

(a)   Decreased Communication with Children

(b)   Reduced Parental Involvement

(c)   Increased Access to Parenting Resources

(d)   Limited children's educational opportunities

Answer: (c) INCREASED ACCESS TO PARENTING RESOURCES

AN EXTRA MINUTE

INCREASED ACCESS TO PARENTING RESOURCES such as online forums, educational websites, and parenting apps all these empowers you with valuable information and support. These resources provide expert advice, diverse perspectives, and practical tips for various parenting challenges. Social media platforms foster community connections, allowing you to share experiences and solutions with others and your own child(ren). This digital age accessibility enhances parenting skills, encourages informed decision-making, and promotes a nurturing environment for your child(ren).

"Your child(ren) will become what you are; so be what you want them to be."
– (David Bly)

9. **What is a common Parenting practice in the 21st Century related to education?**

    (a) Home Schooling

    (b) Military Schooling

    (c) Boarding Schools

    (d) Apprenticeships

Answer: (a) HOME SCHOOLING

AN EXTRA MINUTE

HOME SCHOOLING in the 21st century leverages digital tools and resources to offer a flexible, personalized education. Online curricula, virtual classrooms, and educational apps provide diverse learning opportunities tailored to individual needs. You can extensively access a wealth of teaching materials and connect with home schooling communities to support you.. This modern approach promotes self-directed learning, critical thinking, and adaptability, preparing your kid(s) for future challenges in a dynamic world.

"The greatest gifts you can give your child(ren) are the roots of responsibility and the wings of independence."

– (Denis Waitley)

10. **Which term describes type of Parents who constantly intervene in their child(ren)'s lives to protect them from failures?**

    (a) Tiger Parents

    (b) Helicopter Parents

    (c) Free-range Parents

    (d) Neglectful Parents

Answer: (b) HELICOPTER PARENTS

AN EXTRA MINUTE

HELICOPTER PARENTS usually intervene to protect child(ren) from failures and this may encourage active involvement in their lives to ensure safety and success. You should provide guidance, support, and problem-solving strategies, aiming to prevent mistakes by your child(ren). While well-intentioned, excessive intervention can hinder a child's ability to develop resilience, independence, and critical thinking skills. Balancing protection with allowing child(ren) to experience and learn from setbacks is essential for fostering confidence and long-term growth.

"There is no such thing as a perfect parent. So just be a real one."

– (Sue Atkins)

11. What role does social media play in 21st Century Parenting?

(a) Decreases Family Bonding Time

(b) Provides a Platform for Parenting Communities

(c) Eliminates the need for Face-to-Face Interaction

(d) Increases peer Pressure on Parents

Answer: (b) PROVIDES A PLATFORM FOR PARENTING COMMUNITIES

AN EXTRA MINUTE

PROVIDES A PLATFORM FOR PARENTING COMMUNITIES by offering support, advice, and a sense of belonging. You should actively share experiences, seek guidance, and access diverse perspectives through social group. Platforms like Facebook, Instagram, and Reddit facilitate discussions on various parenting topics, from childcare tips to coping with challenges. This virtual connectivity enables you to build networks, learn from each other, and stay informed about the latest parenting trends and resources.

"Child(ren) are great imitators, so give them something great to imitate."

– (Unknown)

12. Which Parenting Style is known for strict rules and high expectations without emotional warmth?

(a) Authoritative

(b) Permissive

(c) Authoritarian

(d) Neglectful

Answer: (c) AUTHORITARIAN

AN EXTRA MINUTE

AUTHORITARIAN PARENTING is characterized by strict rules, high expectations, and a lack of emotional warmth. It is observed that parents enforce rigid discipline and expect unquestioning obedience and often using punitive measures. This style emphasizes control and compliance over nurturing and open communication. Child(ren) raised in authoritarian households may struggle with self-esteem, fear of failure, and social skills. The lack of emotional support can hinder their ability to develop independence and form healthy relationships.

"Behind every young child who believes in himself is a parent who believed first."
– (Matthew Jacobson)

13. What is one of the benefits of Authoritative Parenting?

(a) High Academic Performance in Child(ren)

(b) Low Self-Esteem in Child(ren)

(c) High Levels of Child Anxiety

(d) Poor Social Skills in Child(ren)

Answer: (a) HIGH ACADEMIC PERFORMANCE IN CHILDREN

AN EXTRA MINUTE

HIGH ACADEMIC PERFORMANCE IN CHILDREN is characterized by warmth and structure and correlates strongly with high academic performance in child(ren). This authoritative style of parenting encourages independence, self-discipline, and effective decision-making skills. Child(ren) raised with clear expectations and nurturing guidance tend to excel academically due to enhanced motivation, confidence, and a positive attitude towards learning. They often develop strong study habits, critical thinking abilities, and resilience in overcoming academic challenges. These factors collectively contribute to sustained academic success and also for preparation for future educational pursuits.

"Each day of our lives we make deposits in the memory banks of our child(ren)."
– (Charles R. Swindoll)

14. What modern tool helps Parents monitor their children's internet usage?

(a) Firewalls

(b) Parental Control Software

(c) Antivirus Programs

(d) Email Filters

Answer: (b) PARENTAL CONTROL SOFTWARE

AN EXTRA MINUTE

PARENTAL CONTROL SOFTWARE offers essential tools for managing chil(ren)'s online activities. It enables parents to monitor and limit screen time, block inappropriate content, and track digital interactions. Such software fosters safer internet browsing, protecting child(ren) from harmful content and online predators. It also promotes healthy device usage habits and encourages balanced screen time. Additionally, parental control software allows you to set educational goals, track progress, and engage in constructive discussions about online safety and responsible digital citizenship with your child(ren).

"It is easier to build strong child(ren) than to repair broken men."

– (Frederick Douglass)

15. Which factor is crucial in shaping 21st Century Parenting Practices?

(a) Economic Downturns

(b) Political Changes

(c) Technological Advancements

(d) Environmental Concerns

Answer: (c) TECHNOLOGICAL ADVANCEMENTS

AN EXTRA MINUTE

TECHNOLOGICAL ADVANCEMENTS significantly shape 21st-century parenting practices by providing innovative tools and resources. Smartphones, apps, and wearable devices offer real-time monitoring of child(ren)'s safety and well-being. Online educational platforms and virtual classrooms also support personalized learning at home. Social media and online communities enable you to connect, share advice, and access diverse parenting resources. These advancements promote informed decision-making, enhance communication, and support you in managing their child(ren)'s development, health, and education more effectively and efficiently.

"Don't worry that child(ren) never listen to you; worry that they are always watching you."

– (Robert Fulghum)

16. What is the primary advantage of Attachment Parenting?

(a) Establishing Strict Rules

(b) Encouraging Independence early on

(c) Building Strong Emotional Bonds

(d) Minimizing Parental Involvement

Answer: (c) BUILDING STRONG EMOTIONAL BONDS

AN EXTRA MINUTE

BUILDING STRONG EMOTIONAL BONDS emphasizes physical closeness, responsive caregiving, and consistent emotional support. Practices like baby wearing, co-sleeping, and extended breastfeeding foster secure attachments, enhancing a child's sense of trust and safety. These strong emotional bonds promote healthy social and emotional development, leading to greater self-esteem, empathy, and resilience. Attachment parenting nurtures a deep, lasting connection, ensuring children feel loved, understood, and valued throughout their growth.

"Child(ren) are made readers on the laps of their parents."
– (Emilie Buchwald)

17. How do 21st Century Parents often communicate with their child(ren)'s teachers?

(a) Phone Calls

(b) Letters

(c) Emails and Online Portals

(d) Face-to-Face Meetings only

Answer: (c) EMAILS AND ONLINE PORTALS

AN EXTRA MINUTE

EMAILS AND ONLINE PORTALS are the most common methods to communicate with your child(ren)'s teachers. This method offers a convenient and efficient way to stay updated on academic progress, classroom activities, and any concerns. It additionally allows for timely exchanges of information, scheduling of meetings, and sharing of resources. By using digital communication tools, you and teachers can maintain a collaborative relationship, ensuring that the child's educational needs are met and any issues are addressed promptly, contributing to the student's overall success.

"A child seldom needs a good talking to as a good listening to."

– (Robert Brault)

18. What is a common issue related to screen time for child(ren)?

(a) Lack of Educational Content

(b) Excessive Exposure leading to Negative Effects

(c) Limited Availability of Devices

(d) Screen Time is Rarely Monitored

Answer: (b) EXCESSIVE EXPOSURE LEADING TO NEGATIVE EFFECTS

AN EXTRA MINUTE

EXCESSIVE EXPOSURE LEADING TO NEGATIVE EFFECTS is common especially in child(ren) who expose themselves to prolonged screen use. Eye strain, sleep disturbances, and reduced physical activity, contributing to obesity and related health issues are common. It can also impact mental health, leading to increased anxiety, depression, and decreased attention span. Social skills may suffer as face-to-face interactions decrease. Therefore, it is essential to balance screen time with other activities to mitigate these adverse effects.

"The best security blanket a child can have is parents who respect each other."

– (Jane Blaustone)

19. Which approach focuses on positive reinforcement and encouragement in Parenting?

(a) Authoritarian

(b) Positive Parenting

(c) Neglectful Parenting

(d) Permissive Parenting

Answer: (b) POSITIVE PARENTING

AN EXTRA MINUTE

POSITIVE PARENTING Positive focuses on reinforcing good behavior and encouraging child(ren) through praise and support rather than punishment. It emphasizes the importance of nurturing a child's self-esteem and emotional well-being by recognizing their achievements and self efforts. By fostering a supportive and loving environment, positive parenting helps child(ren) develop confidence, resilience, and a sense of responsibility. This approach promotes healthy parent-child relationships, encouraging open communication and mutual respect, ultimately leading to well-adjusted and happy child(ren).

"Your children need your presence more than your presents."
– (Jesse Jackson)

20. What is a significant trend in 21st Century Parenting related to family structure?

(a) Increase in Extended Families

(b) Decrease in Adoption Rates

(c) Rise in Single-Parent Households

(d) Increase in Families without Child(ren)

Answer: (c) RISE IN SINGLE – PARENT HOUSEHOLDS

AN EXTRA MINUTE

RISE IN SINGLE-PARENT HOUSEHOLDS has become a significant trend in modern society. This increase is due to various factors, including higher divorce rates, changing societal norms, and the growing acceptance of single parenthood by choice. Single parents face unique challenges, such as balancing work and childcare, financial pressures, and the need for robust support networks. Despite these challenges, many single-parent families thrive, demonstrating resilience and adaptability. They often foster strong bonds, independence, and a sense of responsibility in their child(ren).

"Parenthood: The state of being better chaperoned than you were before marriage."
– (Marcelene Cox)

21. How do modern Parents address Cyberbullying?

(a) Involving Law Enforcement and School Authorities

(b) Removing all Internet Access

(c) Blaming their Child(ren)

(d) Ignoring it

Answer: (a) INVOLVING LAW ENFORCEMENT AND SCHOOL AUTHORITIES

AN EXTRA MINUTE

INVOLVING LAW ENFORCEMENT AND SCHOOL AUTHORITIES in cases of cyberbullying is crucial for ensuring a safe and supportive environment for students. These authorities can investigate incidents, enforce anti-bullying policies, and provide necessary interventions. Their involvement helps hold perpetrators accountable and offers protection to victims. Schools can implement educational programs and workshops on digital citizenship, while law enforcement can offer resources for reporting and dealing with cyberbullying. Collaboration between you parents, educators, and law enforcement is essential in addressing and preventing cyberbullying effectively.

"The sign of great parenting is not the child's behaviour. The sign of truly great parenting is the parent's behaviour."

– (Andy Smithson)

22. What is a common strategy for managing children's use of technology?

(a)   Unrestricted Access

(b)   Scheduled Screen Time

(c)   Total Ban on Devices

(d)   Letting Child(ren) Decide

Answer: (b) SCHEDULED SCREEN TIME

AN EXTRA MINUTE

SCHEDULED SCREEN TIME is an effective strategy for managing child(ren)'s use of technology. By setting specific periods for screen activities, you should ensure a balanced lifestyle that includes physical activity, homework, and family interactions. This approach helps child(ren) develop self-discipline and time management skills. Scheduled screen time also reduces the risk of excessive exposure, which can lead to issues like eye strain and sleep disturbances. Consistent routines foster a healthy relationship with technology, promoting overall well-being.

"To be a good parent, you need to take care of yourself so that you can have the physical and emotional energy to take care of your family."

– (Michelle Obama)

23. Which of the following is a benefit of Co-Parenting in the 21st Century?

(a) Increased Parental Conflict

(b) Better Emotional Support for Child(ren)

(c) Less Involvement in Child(ren)'s Lives

(d) Financial Strain

Answer: (b) BETTER EMOTIONAL SUPPORT FOR CHILDREN

AN EXTRA MINUTE

BETTER EMOTIONAL SUPPORT FOR CHILDREN is crucial in a co-parenting relationship. It fosters a stable and nurturing environment that helps children thrive and also give child(ren) your full attention, showing that their thoughts and feelings are important. Acknowledge and validate their emotions, letting them know it's normal to feel the way they do and show understanding and empathy towards their experiences and feelings. Teach your child(ren) to understand and manage their emotions effectively and demonstrate healthy emotional behavior for children to emulate.

"Raising children is a journey, not a race."

– (Unknown)

24. How has the role of fathers changed in Parenting?

(a)   Fathers are Less Involved in Childcare

(b)   Fathers are Uninvolved in Parenting Decisions

(c)   Fathers Focus only on Financial Support

(d)   Fathers are taking on more Active Parenting Roles

Answer: (d) FATHERS ARE TAKING ON MORE ACTIVE PARENTING ROLES

AN EXTRA MINUTE

FATHERS ARE TAKING ON MORE ACTIVE PARENTING ROLES by getting engaged in their child(ren)'s daily routines, including school drop-offs, homework help, and bedtime rituals and whenever required they are taking paternity leave to bond with their newborns, supporting their partners and participating in early child-rearing. Fathers are involved in their child(ren)'s healthcare, attending pediatric appointments, and promoting healthy lifestyles through physical activities and proper nutrition. Many dads are establishing strong co-parenting relationships, ensuring consistent and supportive environments for their children.

"The goal of parenting is not to create perfect child(ren), but to parent them perfectly."

– (Unknown)

25. What is the impact of Dual-Income Families on Parenting?

(a) Decreased Childcare Options

(b) Increased Reliance on Daycare and Babysitters

(c) Less Financial Stability

(d) More Time Spent with Child(ren)

Answer: (b) INCREASED RELIANCE ON DAY CARE AND BABYSITTERS

AN EXTRA MINUTE

INCREASED RELIANCE ON DAY CARE AND BABYSITTERS has become necessity with more families having both parents working, there is a greater need for reliable childcare solutions and daycare offers opportunities for child(ren) to socialize and interact with peers, enhancing their social skills. There are many other reasons for this arrangement like many daycare centers provide educational activities that support early childhood development and learning.

"Parenting is the easiest thing in the world to have an opinion about, but the hardest thing in the world to do."

– (Matt Walsh)

26. Which practice is essential in Positive Parenting?

(a) Punishing Mistakes Harshly

(b) Setting no Boundaries

(c) Encouraging and rewarding positive behavior

(d) Ignoring Bad Behavior

Answer: (c) ENCOURAGING AND REWARDING POSITIVE BEHAVIOR

AN EXTRA MINUTE

ENCOURAGING AND REWARDING POSITIVE BEHAVIOR is done to reinforce the desired actions and should regularly use positive words and affirmations to encourage good behaviour. Give positive feedback in front of others, boosting the child's confidence and encouraging continued good behaviour and use tangible rewards like stickers, small toys, or treats to celebrate positive behaviour. Showing affection through hugs, high-fives, and smiles to reinforce positive actions.

"There is no job more important than parenting. This I believe."
– (Benjamin Carson)

27. What challenge do Parents face with Remote Learning?

(a) Access to Traditional Classrooms

(b) Managing Children's Focus and Engagement

(c) Reducing Screen Time

(d) Finding Physical Textbooks

Answer: (b) MANAGING CHILDREN'S FOCUS AND ENGAGEMENT

AN EXTRA MINUTE

MANAGING CHILDREN'S FOCUS AND ENGAGEMENT by establishing a consistent daily schedule that includes designated times for learning, play, and rest and also communicate clear expectations about behaviour and tasks, using simple and age-appropriate language. Break down tasks into manageable steps to prevent overwhelm and encourage success and give child(ren) choices within structured limits to promote autonomy and engagement. Provide opportunities for physical activity and movement breaks to enhance focus.

"The way we talk to our children has a lasting impact on their sense of self."

– (Unknown)

28. Which factor contributes to Parenting Stress in the 21st Century?

(a) Lack of Information

(b) Minimal Social Pressures

(c) Decreased Work Demands

(d) Overabundance of Conflicting Parenting Advice

Answer: (d) OVER ABUNDANCE OF CONFLICTING PARENTING ADVICE

AN EXTRA MINUTE

OVER ABUNDANCE OF CONFLICTING PARENTING ADVICE can ultimately empower parents to make informed decisions that best suit their family dynamics and values. You should align advice with your family's values and beliefs about parenting and consider whether the advice applies to your child's age, personality, and specific circumstances. Be confident to accept any advice backed by scientific research and proven outcomes and seek opinions from trusted experts or professionals when unsure.

"Child(ren) learn more from what you are than what you teach."
– (W.E.B. Du Bois)

29. How do Parents often support children's mental health?

(a) Encouraging Open Communication and Seeking Therapy

(b) Ignoring Emotional Issues

(c) Focusing only on Academic Performance

(d) Providing Minimal Emotional Support

> **Answer: (a) ENCOURAGING OPEN COMMUNICATION AND SEEKING THERAPY**

AN EXTRA MINUTE

ENCOURAGING OPEN COMMUNICATION AND SEEKING THERAPY parents can foster a supportive and emotionally healthy environment for their children to thrive and establish an atmosphere where child(ren) feel comfortable expressing their thoughts and feelings without fear of judgment. Parents should practice active listening by giving full attention to what your child is saying, without interrupting or dismissing their concerns. Demonstrate openness and honesty in your own communication with your child, setting an example for healthy dialogue.

"Parenting is not about being perfect. It's about being connected."

– (Unknown)

30. What is a common characteristic of Permissive Parenting?

(a)   High Demands and Low Responsiveness

(b)   Low Demands and High Responsiveness

(c)   High Demands and High Responsiveness

(d)   Low Demands and Low Responsiveness

Answer: (b) LOW DEMANDS AND HIGH RESPONSIVENESS

AN EXTRA MINUTE

LOW DEMANDS AND HIGH RESPONSIVENESS Understanding these aspects of permissive parenting can help parents evaluate if this style aligns with their values and goals for their child(ren)'s upbringing. It's essential to balance responsiveness with setting appropriate boundaries to promote healthy development and well-being. Discipline is typically non-punitive or minimal, with parents opting to reason and negotiate with their child(ren).

"A child's mental health is just as important as their physical health and deserves the same quality of support."

– (Kate Middleton)

31. Which one best describes the concept of "Mindful Parenting"?

(a) Being Constantly Anxious about Children's Safety

(b) Relying on Technology for Parenting Decisions

(c) Allowing Child(ren) Complete Freedom without Guidance

(d) Staying Present and Fully Engaged with Child(ren)

Answer: (d) STAYING PRESENT AND FULLY ENGAGED WITH CHILDREN

AN EXTRA MINUTE

STAYING PRESENT AND FULLY ENGAGED WITH CHILDREN often referred to as mindful parenting, involves being aware and intentional in your interactions and you start giving your child your full attention when interacting, putting aside distractions like phones or other tasks. Understand your child's perspective and emotions, showing empathy in your responses as well as recognize and respect your child's unique qualities, interests, and developmental stage.

"One hundred years from now, it won't matter what kind of car I drove, what kind of house I lived in, how much money I had in the bank, but the world may be a little better because I was important in the life of a child."

– (Forest E. Witcraft)

32. How can Parents encourage healthy eating habits in children?

(a) Forcing Child(ren) to Eat Vegetables

(b) Ignoring Child(ren)'s Dietary Preferences

(c) Offering only Junk Food

(d) Leading by Example and Providing Balanced Meals

Answer: (d) LEADING BY EXAMPLE AND PROVIDING BALANCED MEALS

AN EXTRA MINUTE

LEADING BY EXAMPLE AND PROVIDING BALANCED MEALS helps promoting a positive approach to food, parents can help instill lifelong healthy eating habits in their children. Praise and encourage child(ren) when they choose healthy options or try new foods and teach them about the nutritional benefits of different foods and the importance of balanced meals. Offer nutritious snacks like fruits, vegetables, yogurt, or whole-grain crackers between meals and encourage drinking water throughout the day and limit sugary beverages.

"It is not what you do for your child(ren), but what you have taught them to do for themselves, that will make them successful human beings."

– (Ann Landers)

33. How do Parents support their children's career aspirations?

(a) Providing Guidance and Resources

(b) Discouraging their Goals

(c) Forcing Specific Career Paths

(d) Ignoring their Interests

Answer: (a) PROVIDING GUIDANCE AND RESOURCES

AN EXTRA MINUTE

PROVIDING GUIDANCE AND RESOURCES by exposing child(ren) to a variety of careers by taking them to workplace visits, career fairs, and encourage conversations with professionals in different fields. We should also help child(ren) identify their interests and strengths through hobbies, extracurricular activities, and personality assessments and understanding what they enjoy and are good at can guide their career choices. Connect child(ren) with mentors in their field of interest. Mentors can provide valuable insights, guidance, and networking opportunities.

"If you want your child(ren) to improve, let them overhear the nice things you say about them to others."

– (Haim Ginott)

34. What is an effect of Parental Overprotection?

(a) Increased Resilience in Child(ren)

(b) Decreased Independence and Problem-Solving Skills in Child(ren)

(c) Enhanced Social Skills

(d) Greater Academic Success

Answer: (b) DECREASED INDEPENDENCE AND PROBLEM – SOLVING SKILLS IN CHILD(REN)

AN EXTRA MINUTE

DECREASED INDEPENDENCE AND PROBLEM-SOLVING SKILLS IN CHILD(REN) is an effect of over protection by you. Keep in mind that constant parental intervention can lead to low self-esteem, as child(ren) might feel incapable of achieving things on their own without parental assistance. Child(ren) who grow up overprotected may continue to depend on their parents into adulthood, struggling with independence and self-sufficiency.

"A child's mental health is just as important as their physical health and deserves the same quality of support."

– (Kate Middleton)

35. How do modern Parents handle work-life balance?

(a) Prioritizing Work over Family

(b) Working Excessively Long Hours

(c) Ignoring Family Needs

(d) Finding Flexible Work Arrangements

Answer: (d) FINDING FLEXIBLE WORK ARRANGEMENTS

AN EXTRA MINUTE

FINDING FLEXIBLE WORK ARRANGEMENTS You can pursue consulting or contract work, which often offers flexibility in terms of project timelines and work locations. This can be a good fit for specialized skills and also continue enquiring about flexible leave policies, including the ability to take unpaid leave or personal days when needed for family or personal matters. Use communication and collaboration tools to effectively manage your work tasks while maintaining a flexible schedule.

"The greatest legacy we can leave our child(ren) is happy memories."

– (Og Mandino)

36. What is an impact of social media on children's self-esteem?

(a) Always Positive

(b) Can be Both Positive and Negative, Depending on Usage

(c) Always Negative

(d) No Impact

Answer: (b) CAN BE BOTH POSITIVE AND NEGATIVE, DEPENDING ON USAGE

AN EXTRA MINUTE

CAN BE BOTH POSITIVE AND NEGATIVE, DEPENDING ON USAGE Negative interactions such as cyberbullying can severely damage a child's self-esteem. Hurtful comments, exclusion, and harassment can lead to emotional distress and a diminished sense of self-worth. Child(ren) usually rely on social media for validation, measuring their self-esteem by the number of likes, comments, and followers they receive and this can create a dependence on external approval.

"Child(ren) spell love T-I-M-E."

– (Dr. A. Witham)

37. How can Parents foster resilience in children?

(a) Shielding them from all Difficulties

(b) Solving all their Problems for them

(c) Ignoring their Challenges

(d) Encouraging Problem-Solving and Coping Skills

Answer: (d) ENCOURAGING PROBLEM-SOLVING AND COPING SKILLS

AN EXTRA MINUTE

ENCOURAGING PROBLEM - SOLVING AND COPING SKILLS by this your child(ren) will become more adaptable, able to adjust to new situations and changes with greater ease. Resilient child(ren) tend to have better social skills, as they can navigate interpersonal conflicts and seek support when needed, strengthening their relationships. Child(ren) with effective coping strategies are less likely to experience chronic anxiety, as they feel more equipped to handle the uncertainties and pressures of life.

"The most important thing that parents can teach their children is how to get along without them."

– (Frank A. Clark)

38. What is a common trend in 21st Century Family Structures?

(a) Traditional Nuclear Families only

(b) Diverse Family, including Blended and Single Parent Families

(c) Decreased Diversity in Family Types

(d) Only Extended Families

Answer: (b) DIVERSE FAMILY, INCLUDING BLENDED AND SINGLE - PARENT FAMILIES

AN EXTRA MINUTE

DIVERSE FAMILY, INCLUDING BLENDED AND SINGLE-PARENT FAMILIES often develop greater emotional resilience. They learn to adapt to different circumstances and relationships, which will certainly enhance their ability to handle change and adversity throughout their lives. Blended families, in particular, can offer an expanded network of support. With additional parental figures, siblings, and extended family members, chil(ren) can benefit from a variety of perspectives and guidance.

"The best kind of parent you can be is to lead by example."
– (Drew Barrymore)

39. Which approach is often used to help children develop empathy?

(a) Encouraging Competition

(b) Promoting Personal Discussions about Feelings

(c) Discouraging Emotional Expression

(d) Ignoring Child(ren)'s Social Interactions

Answer: (b) PROMOTING PERSONAL DISCUSSIONS ABOUT FEELINGS

AN EXTRA MINUTE

PROMOTING PERSONAL DISCUSSIONS ABOUT FEELINGS in a safe environment builds trust and strengthens relationships. This connection creates a supportive atmosphere where individuals feel understood and valued, fostering mutual empathy and also improves verbal and non-verbal communication skills. Expressing and interpreting feelings effectively helps individuals to convey empathy more clearly and respond appropriately to others' emotional needs.

"To be in your child(ren)'s memories tomorrow, you have to be in their lives today."
— (Unknown)

40. How do Parents often manage children's extracurricular activities?

(a) Encouraging a Balanced Approach with Time for Rest

(b) Over-Scheduling Multiple Activities

(c) Prohibiting all Extracurricular Activities

(d) Ignoring Child(ren)'s Interests

Answer: (a) ENCOURAGING A BALANCED APPROACH WITH TIME FOR REST

AN EXTRA MINUTE

ENCOURAGING A BALANCED APPROACH WITH TIME FOR REST ensures that your child(ren) have enough time to wind down before bedtime, leading to better sleep quality. Good sleep is vital for growth, learning, and overall health, and it helps your children stay energized and attentive during their activities and also help prevent physical and emotional burnout. A balanced schedule that includes downtime allows your child(ren) to recharge, reducing stress and maintaining their enthusiasm for activities.

"Good parenting requires taking the long view and investing in your child(ren)'s future."

– (Karen Salmansohn)

41. What is a modern Parenting challenge related to child(ren)'s education?

(a) Limited Access to Schools

(b) Managing Remote Learning and Online Education

(c) Lack of Educational Resources

(d) No Involvement in Schooling

Answer: (b) MANAGING REMOTE LEARNING AND ONLINE EDUCATION

AN EXTRA MINUTE

MANAGING REMOTE LEARNING AND ONLINE EDUCATION many parents struggle to balance their own work-from-home responsibilities with supervising their child(ren)'s remote learning. This dual demand can lead to stress and decreased productivity for both parents and child(ren). Not all families have equal access to the necessary technology and reliable internet connectivity for effective remote learning. Technical issues, such as lack of devices or poor internet service, can hinder your child's ability to participate fully in online education.

"Parenting isn't a practice. It's a daily learning experience."
– (Unknown)

42. Which Parenting Style emphasizes unconditional love and acceptance?

(a) Authoritarian

(b) Permissive

(c) Authoritative

(d) Neglectful

Answer: (c) AUTHORITATIVE

AN EXTRA MINUTE

AUTHORITATIVE parenting style emphasizes unconditional love and acceptance and you should focus on praising efforts and accomplishments, which helps your child(ren) internalize positive behaviours and understand that they are valued for who they are, not just for what they do. You, as parent(s) should practice empathy, striving to understand your child(ren)'s perspectives and experiences. This approach fosters mutual respect and acceptance, teaching your child(ren) to approach relationships with compassion and understanding, mirroring the unconditional love they receive from you.

"The best thing a father can do for his child(ren) is to love their mother."

– (John Wooden)

43. How do Parents address children's exposure to inappropriate content online?

(a) Ignoring the Issue

(b) Using Parental Controls and Monitoring Tools

(c) Allowing Unrestricted Access

(d) Relying Solely on Schools to Manage it

Answer: (b) USING PARENTAL CONTROLS AND MONITORING TOOLS

AN EXTRA MINUTE

USING PARENTAL CONTROLS AND MONITORING TOOLS by many parental control apps which offer real-time alerts for suspicious activities or attempts to access restricted content. These alerts provide you with timely information to take immediate action if needed, protecting child(ren) from potential online threats. You can use these tools to guide conversations about responsible internet use, privacy, and the importance of critical thinking when navigating the online world.

"Children are likely to live up to what you believe of them."
– (Lady Bird Johnson)

44. How can Parents support their children's social development?

(a)   Isolating them from Peers

(b)   Encouraging Social Interactions and Friendships

(c)   Focusing only on Academic Achievements

(d)   Ignoring their Social Needs

Answer: (b) ENCOURAGING SOCIAL INTERACTIONS AND FRIENDSHIPS

AN EXTRA MINUTE

ENCOURAGING SOCIAL INTERACTIONS AND FRIENDSHIPS can offer advice on how to navigate social situations, resolve conflicts, and develop healthy relationships. By discussing your child(ren)'s social experiences and offering constructive feedback, you can certainly help them build confidence and improve their interpersonal skills. Make your home a welcoming place for your child(ren)'s friends, you can also encourage social gatherings and foster a sense of community.

"There is no friendship, no love, like that of the parent for the child."
– (Henry Ward Beecher)

45. What is the impact of Gender-Neutral Parenting?

(a) Reinforces Traditional Gender Roles

(b) Reduces Gender Stereotypes and Promotes Equality

(c) Confuses Children's Gender Identity

(d) Has no Impact on Children's Development

Answer: (b) REDUCES GENDER STEREOTYPES AND PROMOTES EQUALITY

AN EXTRA MINUTE

REDUCES GENDER STEREOTYPES AND PROMOTES EQUALITY also emphasizes allowing child(ren) to pursue their own interests and talents, regardless of traditional gender roles. This approach helps child(ren) develop skills and passions based on their personal inclinations rather than societal expectations. Also teaches chil(ren) to treat everyone equally, regardless of gender. This mind set reduces the likelihood of developing prejudiced views and discriminatory behaviours.

"Your greatest contribution may not be something you do,
but someone you raise."
– (Unknown)

46. Which Parenting strategy helps in managing sibling rivalry?

(a) Comparing Siblings Constantly

(b) Ignoring Conflicts

(c) Encouraging Cooperation and Understanding

(d) Favoring one Child over the Other

Answer: (c) ENCOURAGING COOPERATION AND UNDERSTANDING

AN EXTRA MINUTE

ENCOURAGING COOPERATION AND UNDERSTANDING siblings when they successfully complete a task together reinforces the value of cooperation and builds a sense of shared achievement. We also have to ensure that each child receives fair attention, resources, and opportunities helps prevent feelings of favouritism and resentment, which can fuel rivalry.

"Parents are the ultimate role models for children. Every word, movement, and action has an effect. No other person or outside force has a greater influence on a child than the parent."

– (Bob Keeshan)

47. How do modern Parents typically handle child(ren)'s screen time?

(a) Allowing Unlimited Screen Time

(b) Setting Limits and Encouraging other Activities

(c) Prohibiting all Screen Use

(d) Letting Child(ren) Decide their Screen Time

Answer: (b) SETTING LIMITS AND ENCOURAGING OTHER ACTIVITIES

AN EXTRA MINUTE

SETTING LIMITS AND ENCOURAGING OTHER ACTIVITIES and defining how much screen time is allowed each day or week, tailored to each child's age and needs. Consistency in enforcing these limits helps child(ren) understand boundaries. Try to develop a daily routine that includes a balanced mix of activities, such as homework, chores, physical activities, and leisure time. A structured schedule helps child(ren) manage their time better and reduces the likelihood of excessive screen use.

"Your child(ren) are the greatest gift God will give to you, and their souls the heaviest responsibility He will place in your hands."

– (Lisa Wingate)

48. Which of the following is a key component of "Digital Parenting"?

(a) Allowing Unrestricted Internet Access

(b) Prohibiting all Technology Use

(c) Monitoring and Guiding Child(ren)'s Online Activities

(d) Ignoring online Risks

Answer: (c) MONITORING AND GUIDING CHILDREN'S ONLINE ACTIVITIES

AN EXTRA MINUTE

MONITORING AND GUIDING CHILDREN'S ONLINE ACTIVITIES can create a safe and supportive digital environment that helps children navigate the online world responsibly and securely and also by setting clear and consistent rules regarding the use of the internet and digital devices. Make sure your child(ren) understand the guidelines and the reasons behind them. You as parents have to educate your child(ren) about online safety, including the importance of protecting personal information, recognizing cyberbullying, and understanding the risks of interacting with strangers online.

"The only perfect parents are those who don't have kids yet."

– (Dave Willis)

49. What is a modern approach to disciplining children?

(a) Physical Punishment

(b) Positive Discipline and Natural Consequences

(c) Yelling and Shouting

(d) Complete Permissiveness

Answer: (b) POSITIVE DISCIPLINE AND NATURAL CONSEQUENCES

AN EXTRA MINUTE

POSITIVE DISCIPLINE AND NATURAL CONSEQUENCES approach will set clear and consistent expectations for behaviour and you have to ensure that child(ren) understand the rules and the reasons behind them. You have to allow natural consequences to occur and when it is safe and appropriate, let child(ren) experience the outcomes of their actions, which can teach valuable life lessons. You as parents have to use logical consequences that are directly related to the misbehaviour. For example, if a child refuses to clean up their toys, they may lose the privilege of playing with them the next day.

"Being a good parent means being willing to let your child(ren) learn from their mistakes."

– (Michael J. Fox)

50. What is a key aspect of effective communication with teenagers?

(a) Giving Orders without Explanation

(b) Listening Actively and Respectfully

(c) Ignoring their Opinions

(d) Using a Strict Authoritarian Approach

Answer: (b) LISTENING ACTIVELY AND RESPECTFULLY

AN EXTRA MINUTE

LISTENING ACTIVELY AND RESPECTFULLY means that when your teenager speaks, give them your full attention. Put away distractions like phones or laptops, and make eye contact. This shows that you value what they are saying and are fully present in the conversation. As well as reflect back what you've heard to ensure understanding. You can say, "So, what I'm hearing is…" or ask clarifying questions like, "Can you explain more about that?" This demonstrates that you are actively engaged in the conversation and are seeking to understand their point of view fully.

"Child(ren) are not a distraction from more important work. They are the most important work."

– (C.S. Lewis)

51. How do Parents address the issue of bullying?

(a)   Encouraging Children to Fight Back

(b)   Blaming the Victim

(c)   Ignoring the Problem

(d)   Promoting Open Communication and Involving School Authorities

---

Answer: (d) PROMOTING OPEN COMMUNICATION AND INVOLVING SCHOOL AUTHORITIES

AN EXTRA MINUTE

PROMOTING OPEN COMMUNICATION AND INVOLVING SCHOOL AUTHORITIES we have to teach child(ren) about the different forms of bullying (physical, verbal, social, and cyberbullying) and its impacts. Help them understand that bullying is unacceptable and that they should report it if they experience or witness it. Build a cooperative relationship with educators, school counsellors, and administrators. Attend parent-teacher meetings (PTMs) and stay informed about the school's policies on bullying. Encourage your child to communicate with school staff if they face bullying, ensuring they know who to turn to for help.

"Parenting is the most rewarding thing you'll ever do, but it will also be the hardest thing you'll ever do."

– (Unknown)

52. What is a common feature of modern educational tools for Parents?

    (a)   Traditional Textbooks Only

    (b)   Online Resources and Educational Apps

    (c)   Limited Access to Information

    (d)   Outdated Materials

Answer: (b) ONLINE RESOURCES AND EDUCATIONAL APPS

AN EXTRA MINUTE

ONLINE RESOURCES AND EDUCATIONAL APPS frequently offer real-time feedback and assessments, allowing students to track their progress and identify areas for improvement. Immediate feedback helps learners to quickly correct mistakes, reinforce learning, and build confidence. Teachers can also use this data to tailor instruction to meet individual student needs.

"In the end, it's not what you do for your child(ren) but what you've taught them to do for themselves."

— (Ann Landers)

53. How can Parents encourage a love of reading in children?

(a) Providing a Variety of Reading Materials and Setting an Example

(b) Forcing Them to Read Specific Books

(c) Restricting Access to Books

(d) Ignoring their Reading Preferences

Answer: (a) PROVIDING A VARIETY OF READING MATERIALS AND SETTING AN EXAMPLE

AN EXTRA MINUTE

PROVIDING A VARIETY OF READING MATERIALS AND SETTING AN EXAMPLE by reading aloud as a daily routine, even for older child(ren). It can improve their listening skills and encourage a love for stories. Regular trips to the library can be exciting and provide access to a broader range of books. Encourage discussions about books. Encourage discussions about books and ask questions about the stories and characters.

"Parenting is a life-long journey of growth and learning."

– (Unknown)

54. What is a benefit of Parents setting consistent routines for child(ren)?

(a) Increased Anxiety in Child(ren)

(b) Improved Sense of Security and Stability

(c) Less Discipline

(d) Decreased Responsibility

Answer: (b) IMPROVED SENSE OF SECURITY AND STABILITY

AN EXTRA MINUTE

IMPROVED SENSE OF SECURITY AND STABILITY is a positive happening because of consistent routine and it provides a stable and secure environment where child(ren) feel safe and nurtured, promoting emotional well-being. A stable routine can provide a secure base, making it easier for children to handle transitions and unexpected events with confidence.

"The best way to raise children is to help them become who they already are."

– (Meg Meeker)

55. How do Parents address the impact of social media on children's self-image?

(a) Ignoring Social Media Usage

(b) Encouraging Comparison with Others

(c) Allowing Unrestricted Access to Social Media

(d) Discussing the importance of self-esteem and Critical Thinking

---

Answer: (d) DISCUSSING THE IMPORTANCE OF SELF-ESTEEM AND CRITICAL THINKING

AN EXTRA MINUTE

DISCUSSING THE IMPORTANCE OF SELF-ESTEEM AND CRITICAL THINKING ... Social media often leads to comparison with peers, which can affect a child's self-esteem. Seeing idealized images and lifestyles can make child(ren) feel inadequate or insecure about their own lives. Social media is rife with misinformation. Teach your child(ren) to critically evaluate sources and verify information which is crucial to developing their critical thinking skills.

"The best way to keep children at home is to make the home atmosphere pleasant, and let the air out of the tires."

– (Dorothy Parker)

56. What is a modern approach to teaching children about finances?

(a) Keeping them Uninformed

(b) Encouraging Financial Literacy from a Young Age

(c) Managing all Finances for Them

(d) Giving Them Unlimited Money

Answer: (b) ENCOURAGING FINANCIAL LITERACY FROM A YOUNG AGE

AN EXTRA MINUTE

ENCOURAGING FINANCIAL LITERACY FROM A YOUNG AGE by introducing your child(ren) to basic financial concepts such as saving, spending, earning, and budgeting. Teach child(ren) essential financial terms such as bank, interest, debt, and investment. Give child(ren) a regular allowance and guide them on how to budget it. Encourage them to allocate money for different purposes, such as saving, spending, and donating.

"There are no perfect parents, and there are no perfect child(ren), but there are plenty of perfect moments along the way."

– (Dave Willis)

57. How do Parents typically support children's extracurricular interests?

(a) Encouraging Exploration and Participation

(b) Ignoring Their Interests

(c) Forcing Them into Specific Activities

(d) Prohibiting all Extracurricular Activities

Answer: (a) ENCOURAGING EXPLORATION AND PARTICIPATION

AN EXTRA MINUTE

ENCOURAGING EXPLORATION AND PARTICIPATION by exposing your child(ren) to a variety of activities such as sports, music, arts, and clubs. Allow your child(ren) to try different activities without pressure. Encourage them to explore new hobbies and passions to find what they truly enjoy. Attend their events, practices, and performances. Your presence shows support and interest in their activities, making them feel valued and encouraged. Highlight the skills they are developing through their activities, such as teamwork, leadership, time management, and problem-solving.

"Children are not a distraction from more important work.
They are the most important work."
– (Dr. John Trainer)

58. What is an impact of working Parents on children's development?

(a) Negative Impact Only

(b) Positive Role Modeling and Financial Stability

(c) Complete Neglect

(d) Less Opportunity for Education

Answer: (b) POSITIVE ROLE MODELING AND FINANCIAL STABILITY

AN EXTRA MINUTE

POSITIVE ROLE MODELING AND FINANCIAL STABILITY ... Child(ren) observe their parents' dedication and hard work, learning the importance of responsibility, commitment, and perseverance. This instils a strong work ethic and a sense of discipline. Financial stability also allows you to provide for your child(ren)'s basic needs, as well as opportunities for quality education, and enriching experiences and this reduces family stress, creating a more harmonious home environment. Child(ren) in such environments are likely to experience better emotional and psychological well-being.

"Parenting is not for sissies. You have to sacrifice and grow up."

– (Jillian Michaels)

59. How do modern Parents often manage family time?

(a) Prioritizing Individual Activities

(b) Scheduling Regular Family Activities and Meals Together

(c) Ignoring Family Bonding

(d) Allowing Everyone to do Their Own Thing

Answer: (b) SCHEDULING REGULAR FAMILY ACTIVITIES AND MEALS TOGETHER

AN EXTRA MINUTE

SCHEDULING REGULAR FAMILY ACTIVITIES AND MEALS TOGETHER provides many opportunities for open and honest communication. This helps family members to stay connected, share their experiences, and discuss any issues or concerns.Engaging in conversations during these times fosters active listening skills, where family members can express themselves and feel heard and valued. By prioritizing regular family activities and meals, families can create a nurturing and supportive environment that promotes healthy communication, strong relationships, emotional well-being, a healthy lifestyle, and positive behaviour.

"Each day of our lives we make deposits in the memory banks of our children."

— (Charles R Swindoll)

60. What is the role of play in 21st-century Parenting?

(a) Minimizing its Importance

(b) Discouraging Playtime

(c) Focusing Only on Structured Activities

(d) Recognizing play as Essential for Development

Answer: (d) RECOGNIZING PLAY AS ESSENTIAL FOR DEVELOPMENT

AN EXTRA MINUTE

RECOGNIZING PLAY AS ESSENTIAL FOR DEVELOPMENT ... Play encourages child(ren) to think critically and solve problems. Whether through puzzles, building blocks, or imaginative scenarios, they learn to overcome challenges and develop creative solutions. Engaging in play, particularly with others, enhances language development and expands their vocabulary. Play is a natural stress reliever. It provides a safe space for children to release pent-up energy and emotions, reducing anxiety and promoting overall emotional well-being.

"Raising kids may be a thankless job with ridiculous hours,

but at least the pay sucks."

– (Jim Gaffigan)

61. **How do Parents typically address their children's mental health needs?**

(a) Ignoring Emotional Issues

(b) Seeking Professional Help and Promoting Open Discussions

(c) Focusing Only on Physical Health

(d) Discouraging Emotional Expression

> **Answer: (b) SEEKING PROFESSIONAL HELP AND PROMOTING OPEN DISCUSSIONS**

AN EXTRA MINUTE

SEEKING PROFESSIONAL HELP AND PROMOTING OPEN DISCUSSIONS with mental health professionals, such as psychologists, psychiatrists, or counsellors, ensures timely intervention and appropriate treatment. Promoting a healthy lifestyle, including regular exercise, balanced nutrition, adequate sleep, and mindfulness practices, contributes to overall mental well-being and resilience and by open discussions, education, healthy lifestyle practices, and community collaboration.

"Parenting is the greatest act of courage there is. To bring a child into a world you cannot control."

– (Unknown)

62. What is a common approach to discipline in modern Parenting?

(a) Time-outs and Logical Consequences

(b) Physical Punishment

(c) Ignoring Bad Behavior

(d) Allowing Complete Freedom

Answer: (a) TIME – OUTS AND LOGICAL CONSEQUENCES

AN EXTRA MINUTE

TIME - OUTS AND LOGICAL CONSEQUENCES both aim to teach rather than punish. The goal is to help children understand the impact of their behaviour and learn appropriate ways to act. These methods encourage children to reflect on their actions and think about how they can improve. This self-reflection fosters critical thinking and problem-solving skills. Time-outs provide child(ren) with a designated period to calm down and reflect on their behaviour away from distractions. This helps them regain self-control and think about their actions. You should explain why the time-out is being given and ensure the child understands the behaviour that led to it.

"Parenting is the hardest job in the world, and it's the best job in the world."

– (Oprah Winfrey)

63. How do Parents help children develop healthy sleep habits?

(a) Allowing Inconsistent Bedtimes

(b) Establishing a Bedtime Routine and Limiting Screen Time Before Bed

(c) Ignoring Bedtime Routines

(d) Encouraging Late-Night Activities

Answer: (b) ESTABLISHING A BEDTIME ROUTINE AND LIMITING SCREEN TIME BEFORE BED

AN EXTRA MINUTE

ESTABLISHING A BEDTIME ROUTINE AND LIMITING SCREEN TIME BEFORE BED will certainly help to regulate the child's internal clock. Also incorporate calming activities into the bedtime routine, such as reading a book, taking a warm bath, or listening to soft music. This signals to the child that it's time to wind down and prepare for sleep. Ensure your child gets plenty of physical activity during the day. Regular exercise can help children fall asleep faster and enjoy deeper sleep.

"Parenting is a process of teaching our children to be independent, yet still dependent on our love."

– (Unknown)

64. What is the impact of dual-income households on children?

(a) Decreased Educational Opportunities

(b) Higher Rates of Neglect

(c) Less Parental Involvement

(d) Financial Stability and Access to More Resources

Answer: (d) FINANCIAL STABILITY AND ACCESS TO MORE RESOURCES

AN EXTRA MINUTE

FINANCIAL STABILITY AND ACCESS TO MORE RESOURCES allows for better access to healthcare services, including regular check-ups, dental care, and specialized medical treatments. This ensures that your child(ren) maintain good health and receive prompt attention for any medical issues. With more financial resources, families can afford safer and more comfortable living environments. This includes better housing in safer neighbourhoods, access to nutritious food, and overall improved quality of life, which positively impacts child(ren)'s physical and mental well-being.

"Parenting is about guiding your children on the right path."

– (Unknown)

65. How can Parents teach child(ren) about diversity and inclusion?

(a) Encouraging Open-Mindedness and Educating about Different Cultures

(b) Promoting Stereotypes

(c) Ignoring the Topic

(d) Discouraging Interactions with Different Groups

Answer: (a) ENCOURAGING OPEN-MINDEDNESS AND EDUCATING ABOUT DIFFERENT CULTURES

AN EXTRA MINUTE

ENCOURAGING OPEN - MINDEDNESS AND EDUCATING ABOUT DIFFERENT CULTURES and exposing child(ren) to books, movies, music, and art from various cultures can broaden their understanding and appreciation of diversity. You can choose stories and media that feature characters from different backgrounds, highlighting various cultural traditions, languages, and perspectives. Having open and honest conversations about diversity, inclusion, and equality helps child(ren) understand the importance of these values. You should discuss current events, historical examples, and personal experiences that highlight the significance of treating everyone with respect and equality, regardless of their differences.

"Raising kids is part joy and part guerrilla warfare."

– (Ed Asner)

66. What is a modern challenge for Parents in maintaining child(ren)'s physical activity?

(a) Excessive availability of outdoor spaces

(b) Increased screen time and sedentary lifestyle

(c) Lack of interest in sports

(d) Too many physical activities

Answer: (b) INCREASED SCREEN TIME AND SEDENTARY LIFESTYLE

AN EXTRA MINUTE

INCREASED SCREEN TIME AND SEDENTARY LIFESTYLE ... child(ren) are trying to compete with screen time by spending more time engaged in screen-based activities on smartphones, tablets, computers, and television. This digital entertainment often replaces physical playtime, making it challenging for you to encourage active lifestyles and because of safety concerns, urban living, and limited access to safe outdoor spaces can restrict opportunities for child(ren) to engage in outdoor physical activities. You may be finding it difficult to balance the need for safety with the need for physical exercise in these environments.

"There is no such thing as a perfect parent, so just be a real one."

– (Sue Atkins)

67. How do Parents often address their child(ren)'s academic pressures?

(a) Ignoring the Pressures

(b) Adding More Academic Tasks

(c) Providing Support and Encouraging a Balanced Approach

(d) Discouraging Relaxation

Answer: (c) PROVIDING SUPPORT AND ENCOURAGING A BALANCED APPROACH

AN EXTRA MINUTE

PROVIDING SUPPORT AND ENCOURAGING A BALANCED APPROACH which helps alleviate academic pressures by setting realistic and achievable expectations. Emphasizing effort and learning over grades and outcomes can reduce the fear of failure and promote a growth mind set, where child(ren) focus on improvement and personal progress. You support your child(ren) academically by providing resources such as tutoring, study aids, and a conducive learning environment. You should be available to help with homework, offering guidance, and collaborating with school Educators this will certainly ensure that child(ren) have the necessary support to succeed academically without excessive pressure.

The goal of Parenting is not to raise perfect children but to raise happy, healthy, and responsible adults."

– (Unknown)

68. What is an effect of Effective Co-Parenting?

(a) Increased Conflict Between Parents

(b) Consistent Support and Stability for Child(ren)

(c) Reduced Involvement in Child(ren)'s Lives

(d) Lack of Communication

Answer: (b) CONSISTENT SUPPORT AND STABILITY FOR CHILDREN

AN EXTRA MINUTE

CONSISTENT SUPPORT AND STABILITY FOR CHILDREN ensures that your child(ren) receive consistent emotional support from both Parents. This stability helps child(ren) feel secure, reduces anxiety, and fosters a positive emotional environment, which is crucial for their development and well-being. Effective co-parenting minimizes the stress and conflict that child(ren) might otherwise experience in a contentious Parenting situation. A harmonious Co-Parenting relationship creates a peaceful environment, allowing child(ren) to focus on their own growth and activities without being burdened by Parental discord.

"Parenting without a sense of humor is like being an accountant who sucks at math."

– (Amber Dusick)

69. How do Parents support their child(ren)'s emotional intelligence?

(a) Ignoring Their Emotions

(b) Focusing only on Intellectual Development

(c) Teaching Them to Recognize and Express their Feelings

(d) Discouraging Emotional Discussions

Answer: (c) TEACHING THEM TO RECOGNIZE AND EXPRESS THEIR FEELINGS

AN EXTRA MINUTE

TEACHING THEM TO RECOGNIZE AND EXPRESS THEIR FEELINGS and explain why they feel a certain way. For example, saying, "I'm feeling frustrated because I misplaced my keys," shows child(ren) how to identify and articulate emotions. Also by demonstrating healthy ways to express emotions, such as through conversation, art, or physical activity, helps child(ren) learn appropriate ways to express their own feelings. Ask questions like, "How do you think your friend felt when you said that?"

"To be a parent is to sacrifice, to love, to nurture, and to teach."
– (Unknown)

70. How do Parents help children manage stress?

(a) Teaching Coping Strategies and Providing Support

(b) Ignoring their Stress

(c) Adding more Responsibilities

(d) Discouraging any Relaxation

Answer: (a) TEACHING COPING STRATEGIES AND PROVIDING SUPPORT

AN EXTRA MINUTE

TEACHING COPING STRATEGIES AND PROVIDING SUPPORT **by** introducing deep breathing techniques to help child(ren) calm down. You should teach them to take slow, deep breaths in through the nose and out through the mouth and also encourage mindfulness practices like meditation or progressive muscle relaxation to help children focus on the present and reduce anxiety. Encourage child(ren) to express their emotions through creative activities like drawing, painting, or playing a musical instrument. These activities can be therapeutic and provide a constructive outlet for stress.

"There are two things we should give our children: one is roots, and the other is wings."

– (Johann Wolfgang von Goethe)

71. What is an impact of social media on Parenting?

(a) No influence at all

(b) Less opportunity for learning

(c) Decreased parental engagement

(d) Increased access to parenting advice and communities

Answer: (d) INCREASED ACCESS TO PARENTING ADVICE AND COMMUNITIES

AN EXTRA MINUTE

INCREASED ACCESS TO PARENTING ADVICE AND COMMUNITIES ... ... Social media exposes you to a wide range of Parenting Styles, philosophies, and techniques from around the world. This diversity allows you to explore and adopt practices that best suit your family's needs. Platforms like YouTube, Instagram, and Twitter feature advice from child psychologists, pediatricians, and experienced Parents, offering professional insights that can inform Parenting decisions. Social media can also empower you to advocate for issues that matter to them, such as special education, health care, and child safety, by connecting them with like-minded individuals and organizations.

"The way we talk to our children becomes their inner voice."

– (Peggy O'Mara)

72. How do Parents promote responsible internet usage?

(a) Allowing Unrestricted Access

(b) Setting Rules and Discussing Online Safety

(c) Ignoring Internet Activities

(d) Banning all Internet Use

Answer: (b) SETTING RULES AND DISCUSSING ONLINE SAFETY

AN EXTRA MINUTE

SETTING RULES AND DISCUSSING ONLINE SAFETY by teaching your child(ren) about digital citizenship, emphasizing respect, kindness, and responsibility in their online interactions. You have to discuss the impact of their online behaviour on themselves and others. Define specific rules for internet usage, including time limits, acceptable websites, and appropriate online behaviour. Give them clear guidelines which will certainly help your child(ren) understand expectations and the importance of balanced screen time. Spend time online with your child(ren) to guide them through safe and appropriate online behaviour. Co-viewing content and discussing it together can reinforce positive habits.

"Parenting is the easiest thing in the world to have an opinion about, but the hardest thing in the world to do."

— (Matt Walsh)

73. What is the impact of mindfulness on Parenting?

(a) Increases Parental Stress

(b) Reduces Parental Involvement

(c) Enhances Parental Presence and Connection with Child(ren)

(d) Discourages Emotional Expression

Answer: (c) ENHANCES PARENTAL PRESENCE AND CONNECTION WITH CHILDREN

AN EXTRA MINUTE

ENHANCES PARENTAL PRESENCE AND CONNECTION WITH CHILDREN and helps you to manage your own emotions better, allowing them to respond to your child(ren)'s needs more calmly and effectively. This stability creates a more secure and trusting environment for your child(ren). Mindfulness techniques reduce your stress and anxiety, which can improve your overall well-being. Lesser stressed you are more patient and empathetic, fostering a more nurturing and supportive home environment.

"Your children need your presence more than your presents."

– (Jesse Jackson)

74. **How do modern Parents handle the issue of child(ren)'s exposure to violent content?**

   (a)   Monitoring Media Consumption and Discussing the Content

   (b)   Allowing Unrestricted Viewing

   (c)   Ignoring the Issue

   (d)   Encouraging Violent Game

Answer: (a) MONITORING MEDIA CONSUMPTION AND DISCUSSING THE CONTENT

AN EXTRA MINUTE

MONITORING MEDIA CONSUMPTION AND DISCUSSING THE CONTENT by actively monitoring what your child(ren) are watching, playing, or reading. This involves regularly checking the content of TV shows, movies, video games, and online activities. By staying informed, you can pretty well identify and limit exposure to violent content. You also have to teach your child(ren) to think critically about the media they consume. You have to encourage kids to question and analyse the messages in violent content, promoting media literacy. This helps your child(ren) to make informed decisions and recognize the negative effects of violent media.

"The best inheritance a parent can give to their children is a few minutes of their time each day."

– (M. Grundler)

75. What is a modern challenge related to child(ren)'s physical health?

(a) Overabundance of Outdoor Play

(b) Sedentary Lifestyle and Poor Diet

(c) Lack of Technology

(d) Excessive Physical Activities

Answer: (b) SEDENTARY LIFESTYLE AND POOR DIET

AN EXTRA MINUTE

SEDENTARY LIFESTYLE AND POOR DIET characterized by prolonged periods of inactivity, combined with a poor diet high in sugars and fats, can lead to weight gain and obesity in your child(ren). This condition can increase the risk of developing chronic diseases such as diabetes and heart disease and poor nutrition can negatively affect a child's mental health. Regular physical activity is known to boost mood and reduce anxiety and depression. A diet lacking in essential nutrients like omega-3 fatty acids, vitamins, and minerals can also impact brain function and mood regulation.

"Children are the living messages we send to a time we will not see."
– (John F. Kennedy)

76. How can Parents help child(ren) develop time management skills?

(a) Teaching Prioritization and Setting Schedules

(b) Allowing them to Waste Time

(c) Ignoring their Responsibilities

(d) Handling all their Tasks for them

Answer: (a) TEACHING PRIORITIZATION AND SETTING SCHEDULES

AN EXTRA MINUTE

TEACHING PRIORITIZATION AND SETTING SCHEDULES can help child(ren) develop time management skills by establishing a daily routine. This includes setting consistent times for waking up, meals, homework, chores, and bedtime. A structured routine will help your child(ren) understand the importance of organizing their time and build a foundation for effective time management. You should equip children with tools like planners, calendars, or digital apps to help them organize their schedules. Teaching your child(ren) how to use these tools to track assignments, deadlines, and activities can enhance their ability to manage time effectively. Additionally, you can encourage regular check-ins to review schedules and make adjustments as needed, reinforcing the practice of time management.

"A child seldom needs a good talking to as a good listening to."

– (Robert Brault)

77. What is an approach to encouraging creativity in child(ren)?

    (a) Restricting their Activities

    (b) Providing Diverse Opportunities for Creative Expression

    (c) Focusing only on Academic Work

    (d) Ignoring their Interests

Answer: (b) PROVIDING DIVERSE OPPORTUNITIES FOR CREATIVE EXPRESSION

AN EXTRA MINUTE

PROVIDING DIVERSE OPPORTUNITIES FOR CREATIVE EXPRESSION child(ren) get access to different art forms such as drawing, painting, sculpture, music, dance, and drama allows them to explore and express their creativity. Exposure to diverse artistic mediums helps child(ren) discover their own interests and develop new skills, fostering a broader range of creative expression. You should allow your child(ren) free time and space to engage in unstructured creative activities is essential for fostering creativity. This could include setting up a dedicated creative space at home, providing materials like paper, paints, and craft supplies, and allowing children to explore their interests at their own pace. Unstructured time encourages spontaneous creativity and allows children to delve deeply into their imaginative worlds.

"Parenting is the greatest privilege of life."

– (Unknown)

78. How do Parents support child(ren)'s physical activity?

(a) Limiting Physical Play

(b) Encouraging Participation in Sports and Outdoor Activities

(c) Discouraging Exercise

(d) Focusing only on Indoor Activities

Answer: (b) ENCOURAGING PARTICIPATION IN SPORTS AND OUTDOOR ACTIVITIES

AN EXTRA MINUTE

ENCOURAGING PARTICIPATION IN SPORTS AND OUTDOOR ACTIVITIES such as soccer, basketball, swimming, hiking, or cycling. Exposure to a wide range of activities helps child(ren) discover their interests and strengths, making it more likely they'll find a physical activity they enjoy and want to continue. Your children usually emulate your behaviours. By participating in sports and outdoor activities you can set a positive example of an active lifestyle. Family outings like bike rides, nature walks, or playing sports together can be both fun and physically engaging, reinforcing the importance of regular exercise.

"A Parent's love is whole no matter how many times divided."

– (Robert Brault)

79. What is an effect of modern technology on family communication?

(a)   Increased Face-to-Face Interaction

(b)   No Impact on Communication

(c)   Both Enhancing and Hindering Communication Depending on Usage

(d)   Reducing all Forms of Interaction

Answer: (c) BOTH ENHANCING AND HINDERING COMMUNICATION DEPENDING ON USAGE

AN EXTRA MINUTE

BOTH ENHANCING AND HINDERING COMMUNICATION DEPENDING ON USAGE ... ... Modern technology, such as smartphones, video calls, and messaging apps, has made it easier for family members to stay in touch, regardless of distance. This convenience allows families to maintain close connections, share daily experiences, and communicate instantly, fostering a sense of togetherness even when apart. The key to leveraging technology's benefits while minimizing its drawbacks lies in mindful usage. Families can establish guidelines for technology use, such as device-free times or zones, to encourage more focused and meaningful interactions. By being intentional about how and when they use technology, families can enhance communication while avoiding the potential pitfalls of digital distractions.

"Parenting is the ultimate act of love and selflessness."

– (Unknown)

80. How do Parents promote teamwork and cooperation among siblings?

(a) Encouraging Competition

(b) Providing Opportunities for Joint Activities and Responsibilities

(c) Comparing their Achievements

(d) Allowing Conflicts to go Unresolved

Answer: (b) PROVIDING OPPORTUNITIES FOR JOINT ACTIVITIES AND RESPONSIBILITIES

AN EXTRA MINUTE

PROVIDING OPPORTUNITIES FOR JOINT ACTIVITIES AND RESPONSIBILITIES by encouraging siblings to engage in projects and hobbies that require teamwork, such as building a model, gardening, cooking, or crafting. These activities promote cooperation, as child(ren) must work together, share tasks, and communicate effectively to achieve a common goal. You can also create scenarios where siblings need to work together to solve a problem or complete a challenge, such as a puzzle, scavenger hunt, or building something from scratch. These challenges encourage siblings to pool their strengths, think critically, and cooperate to find solutions.

"The most important work you will ever do will be within the walls of your own home."

– (Harold B. Lee)

81. What is a benefit of involving children in household chores?

(a) Decreased Sense of Responsibility

(b) More Time for Parents

(c) Increased Parental Workload

(d) Development of Life Skills and Sense of Contribution

Answer: (d) DEVELOPMENT OF LIFE SKILLS AND SENSE OF CONTRIBUTION

AN EXTRA MINUTE

DEVELOPMENT OF LIFE SKILLS AND SENSE OF CONTRIBUTION comes by involving child(ren) in household chores this teaches them responsibility as they learn to take ownership of specific tasks. This practice also helps them understand the importance of being accountable for their actions and contributes to the overall functioning of the household. Regularly participating in household chores instills a strong work ethic in children. Your child(ren) learn the value of hard work, dedication, and perseverance as they complete tasks, even those that may be less enjoyable. This experience can foster a positive attitude towards work and persistence in other areas of life.

"Parenting is a constant work in progress, a journey of learning and growth."

– (Unknown)

82. How do Parents handle their child(ren)'s use of social media?

(a) Setting Guidelines and Monitoring Usage

(b) Allowing Complete Freedom

(c) Ignoring their Online Activities

(d) Prohibiting all Social Media Use

Answer: (a) SETTING GUIDELINES AND MONITORING USAGE

AN EXTRA MINUTE

SETTING GUIDELINES AND MONITORING USAGE to achieve this you have to set specific guidelines about what is acceptable on social media, including the types of content your child(ren) can post, who they can connect with, and what information they should keep private. Clearly communicating these rules helps your child(ren) understand the boundaries and the reasons behind them. You as Parents should educate your child(ren) about the potential risks of social media, such as cyberbullying, privacy issues, and misinformation. You can also teach them about digital etiquette, including respectful communication, understanding the permanence of online posts, and recognizing the impact of their digital footprint. By providing this education, you are empowering your child(ren) to navigate social media responsibly and safely.

"The best way to love your child(ren) is to spend time with them."
– (Unknown)

83. What is a modern approach to teaching child(ren) about environmental responsibility?

(a) Ignoring Environmental Issues

(b) Encouraging Sustainable Practices and Environmental Awareness

(c) Discouraging Environmental Activities

(d) Limiting their Knowledge about Nature

Answer: (b) ENCOURAGING SUSTAINABLE PRACTICES AND ENVIRONMENTAL AWARENESS

AN EXTRA MINUTE

ENCOURAGING SUSTAINABLE PRACTICES AND ENVIRONMENTAL AWARENESS will only come by setting an example by adopting eco-friendly habits yourself, such as recycling, conserving water and energy, and reducing waste. By demonstrating these behaviours, you definitely show your child(ren) the practical steps they can take to live more sustainably by making these practices a natural part of their daily lives. Encourage your child(ren) to participate in activities like gardening, composting, or joining community clean-up events helps them understand the importance of caring for the environment. These hands-on experiences teach child(ren) about the impact of their actions on the planet and foster a connection with nature.

"The days are long (for Parents), but the years are short."

– (Gretchen Rubin)

84. How do Parents address the issue of online privacy for their child(ren)?

(a) Ignoring Privacy Concerns

(b) Sharing all Personal Information

(c) Allowing Public Profiles

(d) Teaching about Online Privacy and Setting up Privacy Settings

---

Answer: (d) TEACHING ABOUT ONLINE PRIVACY AND SETTING UP PRIVACY SETTINGS

AN EXTRA MINUTE

TEACHING ABOUT ONLINE PRIVACY AND SETTING UP PRIVACY SETTINGS by educating your child(ren) about the potential consequences of oversharing on social media and other online platforms. This includes the risks of posting photos, sharing locations, or divulging details about daily routines. Teach your child(ren) to think critically about what they share online helps them understand how easily information can be accessed and used by others. Create a safe environment for child(ren) to discuss their online experiences encourages them to seek help when they encounter issues like cyberbullying, inappropriate content, or privacy concerns. You should reassure your child(ren) that they can talk about any problems they face online and work together to find solutions, fostering a supportive and informed approach to managing online privacy.

"The best thing you can spend on your children is time."

– (Arnold Glasow)

85. What is an impact of modern Parenting on child(ren)'s self-discipline?

(a) Encouraging Self-Regulation and Responsibility

(b) Decreased Self-Control

(c) Increased Reliance on Parents

(d) No Development of Discipline

Answer: (a) ENCOURAGING SELF-REGULATION AND RESPONSIBILITY

AN EXTRA MINUTE

ENCOURAGING SELF - REGULATION AND RESPONSIBILITY and set clear expectations for behaviour. By demonstrating responsible habits and maintaining consistent routines, they provide child(ren) with a framework for understanding and practicing self-discipline. Also emphasize positive reinforcement over punitive measures encourages child(ren) to develop self-discipline. By rewarding responsible behaviour and self-control, you can help your child(ren) internalize these values and become more intrinsically motivated to act responsibly.

"Children need love, especially when they do not deserve it."

– (Harold Hulbert)

86. How do Parents manage child(ren)'s exposure to advertising?

    (a)   Allowing Unrestricted Exposure

    (b)   Teaching Critical Thinking about Advertising

    (c)   Ignoring Advertising Impact

    (d)   Encouraging them to Follow Ads

Answer: (b) TEACHING CRITICAL THINKING ABOUT ADVERTISING

AN EXTRA MINUTE

TEACHING CRITICAL THINKING ABOUT ADVERTISING and by explaining common advertising techniques, such as emotional appeals, exaggeration, and celebrity endorsements. By understanding these strategies, your child(ren) can better recognize when an ad is trying to influence their emotions or perceptions, allowing them to question its validity and relevance. Also by instilling a habit of skepticism helps your child(ren) critically evaluate advertisements. You should encourage your child(ren) to ask questions like, "What is this ad trying to sell me?" or "Is this product really necessary?" This critical questioning helps your child(ren) develop a more discerning attitude towards advertising.

"It is easier to build strong children than to repair broken men."

– (Frederick Douglass)

87. What is a benefit of promoting a growth mindset in child(ren)?

(a) Fear of Failure

(b) Fixed Attitudes Towards Abilities

(c) Increased Resilience and Willingness to Learn

(d) Decreased Motivation

Answer: (c) INCREASED RESILIENCE AND WILLINGNESS TO LEARN

AN EXTRA MINUTE

INCREASED RESILIENCE AND WILLINGNESS TO LEARN and your child(ren) see challenges as opportunities to learn and grow rather than as threats. This perspective encourages them to tackle difficult tasks with enthusiasm and perseverance, leading to greater resilience in the face of setbacks. Child(ren) with this mindset promote a love of learning for its own sake, rather than for external validation or rewards. Your child(ren) become intrinsically motivated to explore new subjects, develop new skills, and seek knowledge, leading to a lifelong passion for learning.

"Raising children is a labour of love."

– (Unknown)

88. How do Parents support child(ren)'s intellectual development?

(a) Providing Stimulating & Diverse Learning Experiences

(b) Ignoring Educational Activities

(c) Focusing Only on Entertainment

(d) Limiting Educational Resources

Answer: (a) PROVIDING STIMULATING AND DIVERSE LEARNING EXPERIENCES

AN EXTRA MINUTE

PROVIDING STIMULATING AND DIVERSE LEARNING EXPERIENCES and by exposing your child(ren) to a wide range of subjects—from Science and Math to Arts and Humanities—broadens their understanding of the world. This diversity in learning experiences will certainly help your child(ren) discover their passions and develop a well-rounded intellect, making them more adaptable and open-minded. Also by encouraging creative activities like drawing, music, storytelling, or imaginative play stimulates cognitive and emotional development. Creative expression helps your child(ren) develop language skills, emotional intelligence, and innovative thinking, all of which contribute to their intellectual growth.

"Parenting is not a competition. It's a journey we are all on together."

– (Unknown)

89. What is a common feature of Parenting in the digital age?

(a) Integrating Technology while Teaching Digital Literacy

(b) Avoiding Technology Use

(c) Limiting all Technological Interactions

(d) Ignoring Digital Advancements

Answer: (a) INTEGRATING TECHNOLOGY WHILE TEACHING DIGITAL LITERACY

AN EXTRA MINUTE

INTEGRATING TECHNOLOGY WHILE TEACHING DIGITAL LITERACY includes teaching child(ren) about responsible and respectful online behaviour. This encompasses understanding the impact of their digital footprint, practicing good online manners, and being mindful of how they interact with others on social media and other platforms. You, as Parent, should leverage technology as a tool for learning and creativity. Educational apps, online courses, and interactive games can enhance learning experiences, making education more engaging and accessible. You have to encourage your child(ren) to use technology for creative pursuits, such as coding, digital art, or video production.

"The best way to teach children about money is to not have any."

– (Katharine Whitehorn)

90. How do Parents handle the issue of childhood obesity?

(a) Ignoring Dietary Habits

(b) Discouraging Exercise

(c) Encouraging Junk Food Consumption

(d) Promoting Healthy Eating and Physical Activity

Answer: (d) PROMOTING HEALTHY EATING AND PHYSICAL ACTIVITY

AN EXTRA MINUTE

PROMOTING HEALTHY EATING AND PHYSICAL ACTIVITY and by reducing the intake of sugary drinks, snacks, and processed foods is essential in managing weight. You have to educate your child(ren) about the negative health impacts of excessive sugar and processed foods, guiding them to make healthier choices like water, fresh fruits, and whole foods. Encourage regular physical activity for maintaining a healthy weight and overall well-being. Counsel your child(ren) to participate in a variety of activities, such as sports, dance, cycling, or simply playing outdoors. Making physical activity a fun and regular part of family life will certainly help your child(ren) develop a positive attitude towards exercise.

"Parenting is not for the faint of heart."

– (Unknown)

91. What is an effect of Parental involvement in child(ren)'s education?

(a) Lower Academic Performance

(b) Higher Academic Achievement and Motivation

(c) Increased Stress

(d) Less Interest in Learning

Answer: (b) HIGHER ACADEMIC ACHIEVEMENT AND MOTIVATION

AN EXTRA MINUTE

HIGHER ACADEMIC ACHIEVEMENT AND MOTIVATION because Parents often establish routines and provide a structured environment conducive to learning. This includes setting aside time for homework, providing a quiet study space, and monitoring academic progress. Such an environment will help your child(ren) develop good study habits and time management skills, contributing to better academic performance. Your active involvement can foster a love of learning by making education a shared and enjoyable experience. You should engage your child(ren) in educational activities outside of school, such as reading together, visiting museums, or exploring educational games and hobbies. This broadens child(ren)'s horizons and nurtures a lifelong curiosity and passion for learning.

"Parenting is the ultimate long-term investment."
– (Unknown)

92. How can Parents foster a love of learning in child(ren)?

(a) Restricting Access to Educational Resources

(b) Providing Diverse Learning Opportunities and Encouraging **Curiosity**

(c) Ignoring Academic Achievements

(d) Forcing Child(ren) to Study without Breaks

Answer: (b) PROVIDING DIVERSE LEARNING OPPORTUNITIES AND ENCOURAGING CURIOSITY

AN EXTRA MINUTE

PROVIDING DIVERSE LEARNING OPPORTUNITIES AND ENCOURAGING CURIOSITY and by a positive and supportive environment which is essential for nurturing a love of learning. You should celebrate your child(ren)'s achievements, encourage them to take on new challenges, and provide guidance without pressure. This supportive approach will certainly help your child(ren) feel confident in their abilities and motivate them to explore new subjects with enthusiasm. You pretty well know that your child(ren) often emulate your behaviors and attitudes. You have to demonstrate enthusiasm for learning, whether through reading, engaging in new hobbies, or discussing interesting topics, and inspire your child(ren) to do the same. This modeling shows that learning is a lifelong pursuit, not limited to the classroom.

"The most important work you will ever do will be within the walls of your own home."

– (Harold B. Lee)

93. What is a primary focus of 21st-century Parenting?

(a) Strict Discipline and Punishment

(b) Nurturing Emotional Intelligence and Resilience

(c) Encouraging Competitive Behaviour

(d) Limiting Child(ren)'s Exposure to Technology

Answer: (b) NURTURING EMOTIONAL INTELLIGENCE AND RESILIENCE

AN EXTRA MINUTE

NURTURING EMOTIONAL INTELLIGENCE AND RESILIENCE contribute to better mental health by equipping child(ren) with the tools to cope with stress, anxiety, and setbacks. You should encourage practices like mindfulness, self-reflection, and positive self-talk to foster a healthy emotional state. Emotional intelligence skills such as self-regulation, motivation, and social skills are linked to better academic performance and career success. You should also emphasize the importance of perseverance, goal-setting, and emotional regulation to help their children achieve their long-term goals.

"Child(ren) are not a distraction from more important work.
They are the most important work."
— (Dr. John Trainer)

94. How do modern Parents typically approach child(ren)'s education?

(a) Leaving all educational decisions to schools

(b) Involvement in learning activities and advocating for their children

(c) Ignoring academic progress

(d) Discouraging curiosity and exploration

Answer: (b) INVOLVEMENT IN LEARNING ACTIVITIES AND ADVOCATING FOR THEIR CHILD(REN)

AN EXTRA MINUTE

INVOLVEMENT IN LEARNING ACTIVITIES AND ADVOCATING FOR THEIR CHILD(REN) by attending parent-teacher meetings, volunteering for school events, and participating in Parent associations. This involvement helps you stay informed about your child(ren)'s progress and the school's educational practices, enabling them to support your child(ren)'s learning more effectively. ***You should*** actively assist your child(ren) with homework and school projects. This support can range from providing a conducive study environment and resources to offering guidance and encouragement. By being involved, you help reinforce the lessons learned at school and demonstrate the importance of education.

"To be in your child(ren)'s memories tomorrow,

you have to be in their lives today."

– (Unknown)

95. What is a characteristic of digital Parenting?

(a) Allowing unrestricted internet access

(b) Monitoring and guiding online activities

(c) Ignoring children's online behavior

(d) Banning all technology use

Answer: (b) MONITORING AND GUIDING ONLINE ACTIVITIES

AN EXTRA MINUTE

MONITORING AND GUIDING ONLINE ACTIVITIES by prioritizing educating their child(ren) about online safety, including the importance of privacy, recognizing and avoiding cyberbullying, and understanding the potential risks of sharing personal information. You should engage in ongoing conversations about the digital world, helping your child(ren) develop critical thinking skills and the ability to navigate the internet safely. Digital Parents foster an environment of open communication where child(ren) feel comfortable discussing their online experiences, concerns, and questions. By maintaining a non-judgmental and supportive approach, you should guide your child(ren) through digital challenges and help them make informed decisions about their online activities.

"Parenting is the most rewarding thing you'll ever do, but it will also be the hardest thing you'll ever do."

– (Unknown)

96. How can Parents promote healthy sleep habits in child(ren)?

(a) Allowing irregular bedtime routines

(b) Establishing a consistent bedtime routine and limiting screen time

(c) Encouraging late-night activities

(d) Ignoring sleep patterns

Answer: (b) ESTABLISHING A CONSISTENT BEDTIME ROUTINE AND LIMITING SCREEN TIME

AN EXTRA MINUTE

ESTABLISHING A CONSISTENT BEDTIME ROUTINE AND LIMITING SCREEN TIME by recognizing that screen time can interfere with the production of melatonin, the hormone responsible for sleep, you have to limit the use of electronic devices such as TVs, tablets, and smartphones at least an hour before bedtime. They create screen-free zones in bedrooms and encourage alternative calming activities instead. You should talk to your child(ren) about the benefits of good sleep and how it impacts their mood, energy levels, and overall health. By explaining the reasons behind the bedtime routine and screen time limits, parents help child(ren) understand the value of these practices, encouraging them to take ownership of their sleep habits.

"In the end, it's not what you do for your child(ren) but what you've taught them to do for themselves."

– (Ann Landers)

97. What is an effect of encouraging play in child(ren)'s development?

(a)   Stifling creativity

(b)   Enhancing cognitive and social skills

(c)   Limiting physical activity

(d)   Decreasing social interaction

Answer: (b) ENHANCING COGNITIVE AND SOCIAL SKILLS

AN EXTRA MINUTE

ENHANCING COGNITIVE AND SOCIAL SKILLS ... you should note that play stimulates your child(ren)'s creativity and imagination as they invent scenarios, roles, and rules. This imaginative play helps develop problem-solving skills and cognitive flexibility, allowing your child(ren) to think outside the box and come up with innovative solutions to challenges. Through play, your child(ren) engage in conversations, negotiate roles, and articulate their thoughts and ideas. This interaction enhances their vocabulary, language comprehension, and communication skills, which are critical for effective social interaction and academic success.

"Parenting is a life-long journey of growth and learning."
– (Unknown)

98. How do Parents typically handle child(ren)'s exposure to media violence?

(a) Allowing unrestricted access to violent content

(b) Monitoring media consumption and discussing content with children

(c) Ignoring the issue of media influence

(d) Encouraging violent video games

Answer: (b) MONITORING MEDIA CONSUMPTION AND DISCUSSING CONTENT WITH CHILDREN

AN EXTRA MINUTE

MONITORING MEDIA CONSUMPTION AND DISCUSSING CONTENT WITH CHILDREN simultaneously you should establish rules about what types of media are appropriate for your child(ren) to watch. You have to set age-appropriate limits on movies, TV shows, video games, and online content to minimize exposure to violent material. These guidelines help create a safe media environment. To monitor and restrict access to violent content, you should utilize your control features available on devices, streaming services, and gaming consoles. These tools allow you to block or filter out inappropriate content, ensuring your child(ren) only access age-appropriate media.

"The best way to raise child(ren) is to help them become who they already are."

– (Meg Meeker)

99. What is a modern approach to teaching financial responsibility to child(ren)?

(a) Keeping financial matters secret from children

(b) Teaching financial literacy and involving children in budgeting

(c) Ignoring financial discussions

(d) Giving children unlimited spending money

Answer: (b) TEACHING FINANCIAL LITERACY AND INVOLVING CHILDREN IN BUDGETING

AN EXTRA MINUTE

TEACHING FINANCIAL LITERACY AND INVOLVING CHILDREN IN BUDGETING by introducing basic concepts such as saving, spending, and earning. Simple activities like using a piggy bank or playing money-related games help child(ren) understand the value of money and the importance of managing it wisely. You should remember to provide your child(ren) with a regular allowance, using it as an opportunity to teach budgeting skills. You also have to encourage child(ren) to allocate their allowance into different categories such as saving, spending, and giving. This practice helps your child(ren) learn to prioritize and manage their money effectively.

"The greatest legacy we can leave our children is happy memories."

– (Og Mandino)

100. How do Parents typically support child(ren)'s emotional well-being?

(a) Ignoring emotional needs

(b) Encouraging open expression of feelings and seeking professional help if needed

(c) Discouraging emotional discussions

(d) Punishing emotional outbursts

Answer: (b) ENCOURAGING OPEN EXPRESSION OF FEELINGS AND SEEKING PROFESSIONAL HELP IF NEEDED

AN EXTRA MINUTE

ENCOURAGING OPEN EXPRESSION OF FEELINGS AND SEEKING PROFESSIONAL HELP IF NEEDED and foster an environment where child(ren) feel safe to express their emotions without fear of judgment or criticism. By listening attentively and validating their feelings, you should help your child(ren) feel understood and supported, which is crucial for their emotional development. You have to lead by example, demonstrating how to express emotions in a healthy and constructive manner. By openly discussing their own feelings and coping strategies, you provide a model for your child(ren) to follow, teaching them that it is normal and acceptable to talk about their emotions.

"Raising children is a labour of love."

– (Unknown)

Purchase the whole copy at

Amazon IN: https://amzn.in/d/5Ebw62Y

Amazon US: https://a.co/d/8RcUCxj

Amazon UK: https://amzn.eu/d/0vsrGeW

Flipkart: https://dl.flipkart.com/s/enAeiXNNNN

Notionpress: https://notionpress.com/in/read/100-ten-commandments-for-educators